S0-CEZ-551

© 2000 by Barbour Publishing, Inc.

ISBN 1-57748-994-2

All rights reserved. No part of this publication may be reproduced or transmitted in any form or by any means without written permission of the publisher.

All Scripture quotations, unless otherwise noted, are taken from the King James Version of the Bible.

Scripture quotations marked NIV are taken from the HOLY BIBLE, NEW INTERNATIONAL VERSION ®. NIV ®. Copyright © 1973, 1978, 1984 by International Bible Society. Used by permission of Zondervan Publishing House. All rights reserved.

Scripture quotations marked TLB are taken from *The Living Bible* copyright © 1971. Used by permission of Tyndale House Publishers, Inc., Wheaton, Illinois 60189. All rights reserved.

Cover design by Steve Bailey.

The selection by Donna Lange is used with the author's permission.

Published by Humble Creek, P.O. Box 719, Uhrichsville, Ohio 44683

Printed in China.
5 4 3 2 1

ON YOUR
Birthday

A CELEBRATION OF YOUR SPECIAL DAY

written and compiled by
Ellyn Sanna

HUMBLECREEK
INSPIRATION FOR LIFE

On your birthday—and always—
I wish for you. . .

• joy in each passing year;

• the knowledge that you are loved;

• new adventures;

• a sense of achievement as you become the person God made you to be;

• a growing ability to love and be loved;

• a deeper closeness with God;

• and, most of all, a deep understanding of your place in God's eternal kingdom.

CELEBRATE THE YEARS!

The old has gone,
the new has come!

2 CORINTHIANS 5:17 NIV

Experience is a jewel.

WILLIAM SHAKESPEARE

I wish you joy in each passing year. . .

"It is better to be seventy years young than forty years old!"

OLIVER WENDELL HOLMES;

REPLY TO INVITATION FROM JULIA WARD HOWE

TO HER SEVENTIETH BIRTHDAY PARTY, 1889

. . .

To me, fair friend, you never can be old,
For as you were when first your eye I ey'd,
Such seems your beauty still.

WILLIAM SHAKESPEARE

. . .

Wait for that wisest
of all counselors, Time.

PERICLES

Time's Gifts

My twelve-year-old is looking forward to being a "real" teenager next year, and my nine-year-old can't wait to be "double digits." Meanwhile, I have to admit I don't feel quite the same sense of anticipation about my next birthday.

Why is it that children celebrate their birthdays with joy and triumph, but adults feel sadness and embarrassment as they are forced to claim a larger number with each year? The reason has to do, I think, with our culture's attitude about growing older: Up to about age twenty-five, the added years are welcomed—but for the next sixty-five years or so, we act as though the passage of time were a sad secret, a source of shame and regret. And then in our nineties, if we're so fortunate, we're once more "allowed" to feel pride in our ages.

How silly! Celebrate your years right now. Be grateful for all the gifts time has given you, for just as ripe fruit is sweeter than green, you, too, are growing better with age. God has meaning and purpose for each season of your life—and with each birthday, you can celebrate all He's taught you.

Time wasted is existence; used, is life.

EDWARD YOUNG

. . .

Not even the tiny dewdrops lack the attention of the Lover of all. Shall I then think of any detail of my earthly life, even so little a thing as the minute of one of my hours, as without meaning?

ELISABETH ELLIOT

. . .

*Make use of time,
let not advantage slip;
Beauty within itself
should not be wasted.*

WILLIAM SHAKESPEARE

Experience is the mother of truth;
and by experience we learn wisdom.

WILLIAM SHIPPEN, JR.

. . .

Go ahead. After all,
it's your birthday. Celebrate!

. . .

This is the day the Lord has made.
We will rejoice and be glad in it.

PSALM 118:24 TLB

A DAY FOR FAMILIES
AND FRIENDS

Every experience God gives us,
every person He puts in our lives,
is the perfect preparation for the future
that only He can see.

CORRIE TEN BOOM

. . .

The human family is our best illustration of how each person
grows in his unique potentialities by sharing in
the loving care of a society of other persons.

DANIEL DAY WILLIAMS

A Song of Love

Like many extended families, my parents, siblings, and our children can't always celebrate birthdays together. But we still have our favorite birthday traditions—and of them all, my favorite is celebrated early on the birthday morning.

This year was no different. I crawled out of bed, tied my terrycloth robe, and scuffed into the kitchen for my morning routine. Like every other day, I lined slices of bread on the counter for a variety of sandwiches. As I finished packing lunches, one by one my children entered the kitchen. "Happy birthday, Mom," they each said. They gave me birthday hugs. My husband gave me a kiss.

And then the phone rang. This was it, the phone call, the moment I'd been waiting for. "Happy birthday to you, happy birthday to you," sang my parents' voices in my ear. "Happy birthday, dear Donna, happy birthday to you." They ended in two-part harmony.

I could feel my grin spread across my face. My birthday wouldn't be the same without my parents' birthday song. Even when we can't be together later in the day, my siblings and I always get a phone call on our birthday mornings—and on our parents' birthdays, we do the same for them. The sound of our voices singing in unison tells us each that we are loved and cherished, on our birthdays and always.

When my children are grown and on their own, "the phone call" is one tradition I plan to continue.

DONNA LANGE

. . .

Happy birthday!
You are loved so much.

NEW ADVENTURES
EVERY YEAR

The important thing is this:
To be able at any moment to sacrifice what we are
for what we could become.

CHARLES DU BOIS

I wish you new adventures
in the coming year. . .

. . .

A Spirit of Adventure

When I watched my toddlers as they grew, their daring and bravery always impressed me. They pressed forward into life so eagerly, learning new ways to move, new methods of communication, and new foods to enjoy. From the moment they got up every morning, life seemed to be one great adventure of new experiences and sensations.

Somewhere along the way, though, most of us lose our sense of adventure. Instead, we cling to what's familiar. We're afraid to try out new ways of interacting and living and being. Change frightens us.

And yet if we let it, change almost always helps us grow. Change brings into our lives new joys, new ways of understanding, new closeness to God and others.

And so I wish for you a spirit of joy and confidence as you move into your new year.

Total Security

Children who have the assurance to run toward life with open arms do so because they have complete confidence that they are loved. They know if they should fall, loving arms will pick them up. They never doubt that when they cry, someone will care for them and comfort them.

May you have that same knowledge, today and always. Take risks, brave the unknown, accept the challenge of tomorrow —knowing you are completely, absolutely loved by God. If you should fall, His arms will sweep you up; and if you cry, His love will comfort you.

. . .

May your year be full
of new adventures.
And may they all bring you joy!

REJOICE IN THE PERSON
YOU'RE BECOMING

We are the clay, and thou our potter;
and we are all the work of thy hand.

ISAIAH 64:8

. . .

The saints are not to remain undeveloped,
always mere buds and blossoms.
We should grow in grace. . . .

CHARLES SPURGEON

I wish for you today
a sense of achievement
as you grow into the person
God wants you to be. . .

. . .

For He regards men not as they are merely, but as they shall be; not as they shall be merely, but as they are now growing, or capable of growing, towards that image after which He made them that they might grow to it. Therefore a thousand stages, each in itself all but valueless, are of inestimable worth as the necessary and connected gradations of an infinite progress.

GEORGE MACDONALD

. . .

The strongest principle of growth
lies in the human choice.

GEORGE ELIOT

Savor the Freedom

A child understands that each passing year means new accomplishments, new freedoms, new abilities. But as adults, we sometimes look at the passing years as robbers who will steal rather than give to us.

Without a doubt, the years do bring changes. We can spend our time lamenting that fact—or we can be like the child who lets the old methods drop away to make room for the new. Think about it. A toddler can spend her time crying because her mother will no longer carry her—or she can run and dance because her own legs now carry her.

Today, on the anniversary of your birth, take time to look at your life. Don't count the things you've "lost." Instead, savor all the ways today you, too, are free to dance.

To exist is to change,
to change is to mature,
to mature is to go on
creating oneself endlessly.

HENRI BERGSON

. . .

Not a having and a resting,
but a growing and a becoming is the character of perfection.

MATTHEW ARNOLD

Consider the lilies how they grow.

LUKE 12:27

. . .

Grow, by all means. . .but grow,
I beseech you, in God's way,
which is the only effectual way.

HANNAH WHITALL SMITH

. . .

Time ripens all things.

MIGUEL DE CERVANTES

Always Upward

"Are you all grown up now?" my son asked me one day.

"I suppose," I told him. But lately I've been thinking about his question. And I think I need to change my answer.

I'm not "all grown up" after all. Every year, I learn new ways to get along better with my family and friends. New ideas broaden my horizons. People come into my life who help me see new ways of looking at the world. And every year, I grasp a little bit more of God and His love.

But no matter how much I learn, there's always more. I've noticed my eighty-three-year-old father is stilling growing, too, so I suspect we're never done with growing, not in this life— and maybe not in the next, either.

. . .

With each year that passes,

may you grow up. . .

and up. . .and up!

MORE YEARS. . .
MORE LOVE

Those who love deeply never grow old.

SIR ARTHUR WING PINERO

This year, and every year,
may you find a deeper capacity
to love and be loved. . .

. . .

Instead of allowing yourself to be unhappy, just let your love grow as God wants it to grow. Seek goodness in others. Love more persons more. . .more unselfishly, without thought of return. The return, never fear, will take care of itself.

HENRY DRUMMOND

Practice Makes Perfect

We don't have to grow more loving as we grow older. In fact, if we so choose, quite the opposite can happen: We can become pinched, bitter, irritable people—the sort of crabby, crusty individuals who have no joy themselves and give none to others.

But if, instead, we commit ourselves each year to loving more, if we open ourselves more and more to the love of God and others, then we will find love working its ways in our hearts and in our lives. Like anything else, love grows more easy with practice.

. . .

If only I may grow
    firmer,
    simpler,
    quieter,
    warmer.

DAG HAMMARSKJOLD

GROW CLOSER TO GOD
WITH THE PASSING YEARS

Grow in grace,
and in the knowledge of our Lord
and Saviour Jesus Christ.

2 PETER 3:18

. . .

Keep your face upturned to Him as the flowers do to the sun.
Look, and your soul shall live and grow.

HANNAH WHITALL SMITH

May you find this year
an ever-deeper closeness to God. . .

. . .

Let time flow by, with which we
flow on to be transformed into
the glory of the children of God.

FRANCIS DE SALES

One Day. . .

In Paul's first letter to the Corinthians he writes, "When I was a child, I talked like a child, I thought like a child, I reasoned like a child. When I became a man, I put childish ways behind me. Now we see but a poor reflection. . .then we shall see face to face. Now I know in part; then I shall know fully, even as I am fully known" (1 Corinthians 13:11–12, NIV). Clearly, Paul is saying that as we grow older, we also come to understand more of the God we love.

As a young adult, I thought I had God all figured out. Since then, though, I've found that God has a disconcerting habit of shattering again and again my neat little image of Him. I suspect that even a thousand birthdays would be too short a time to fathom God.

Thank God I have eternity.

. . .

In the year that comes. . .
take time for God.

ETERNAL BIRTHDAYS

Fill up the hours with what will last:
Buy up the moments as they go.
The life above, when this is past,
Is the ripe fruit of life below.

HORATIUS BONAR

. . .

The intimate union with Christ. . .
makes the Christian life
an eternal life lived
in the midst of time.

C. HAROLD DODD

On your birthday, and always,
my deepest prayer is that you'll
understand your place
in God's eternal kingdom. . .

. . .

All we need to experience is that we have
"passed out of death into life."
What we need to know takes all time and eternity.

OSWALD CHAMBERS

. . .

God dwells in eternity, but time dwells in God.
He has already lived all our tomorrows
as He has lived all our yesterdays.

A. W. TOZER

A Heavenly Birthday Party

"In heaven," my oldest daughter used to tell me, "we get to be any age we want, whenever we want." The thought pleases me; I like to think I could look at heaven with the innocence and wonder of my four-year-old self; I could gasp with the silly giggles of my adolescence; or I could enjoy the wisdom achieved in eighty years of living.

I don't know what heaven will be like, of course. But I do believe we carry inside us all the birthdays of our lives. And by the power of Christ, the gifts of each year—those lasting, eternal treasures like wonder and joy and wisdom—will accompany us when we go into God's presence to live forever.

Maybe we fear the passing of time because it makes us realize that the things of this world never last. But when we celebrate our spiritual birthday in Christ, we realize our place in His kingdom is solid. . .permanent. . .forever.

. . .

I will come forth as gold.

JOB 23:10 NIV

. . .

Rejoice!
The kingdom of heaven
celebrates your birthday!

God bless thy year!
Thy rest, thy traveling about,
The rough, the smooth,
The bright, the drear,
God bless thy year!

ANONYMOUS